DRAWING CHIBI

LEARN HOW TO DRAW KAWAII PEOPLE, ANIMALS, AND OTHER UTTERLY CUTE STUFF

ILLUSTRATIONS BY TESSA CREATIVE ART

TEXT BY KIERRA SONDEREKER

ULYSSES PRESS

Published in the US by:
ULYSSES PRESS
P.O. Box 3440
Berkeley, CA 94703
www.ulyssespress.com

ISBN: 978-1-64604-093-3
Library of Congress Control Number: 2020936415

Printed in the United States
10 9 8 7 6 5 4 3

Acquisitions editor: Keith Riegert
Managing editor: Claire Chun
Editor: Kate St.Clair
Proofreader: Renee Rutledge
Front cover design: Flor Figueroa
Artwork: Tessa Creative Art
Interior design: what!design @ whatweb.com
Layout: Jake Flaherty

CONTENTS

CHIBI PEOPLE SKILLS 87

ADVANCED CHIBI PEOPLE 105

SIMPLE
KAWAII STYLE

DIXIE (THE CHICK)

STEP 1
Draw a round, slightly lumpy body that is flat on the bottom. Give Dixie some ruffled tail feathers on the bottom right side.

STEP 2
Add some dark eyes set off to the left and above the midway point of the body. Draw small eyebrows and a fluffy wing. At the top of the head, sketch a tuft of feathers. Erase to make two white spots in each eye.

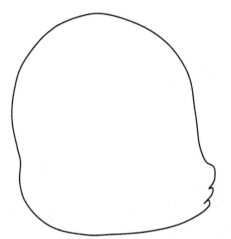

Practice a Couple of Dixies!

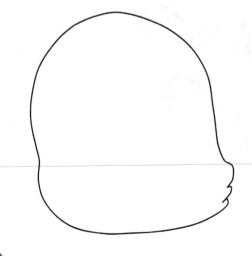

STEP 3

Erase the lines at the top of the head that overlap with the tuft of feathers. Draw a rounded beak (like a sideways heart) below and in between the eyes. Sketch small feet at the bottom. Put one foot in front of the body and one behind.

STEP 4

Remove the body line that the right foot is now covering. To complete Dixie, add some light shading.

SPLISH (THE KOI)

STEP 1
Start by drawing a body that looks like a teardrop lying on its side.

STEP 2
Sketch some tail fins. Then add more fins by drawing some ridges at the top of the body, with part of the ridge in the middle extending slightly into the body. Add more jagged ridges on the bottom curve of Splish's body.

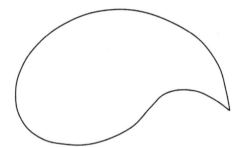

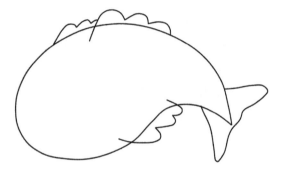

Draw More Splishes!

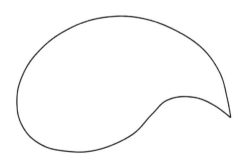

STEP 3 Erase the top body line so the fins starting in the center are connected to the body. Do the same for the tail fins and the lower body fins. Draw dark, round eyes with a small white dot near the top.

STEP 4 Give Splish some shading on his upper body and fins. He's ready to make a splash!

SPECKLE (THE GIRAFFE)

STEP 1

Start by drawing a small oval with an arch on top, or what looks like an upside-down acorn.

STEP 2

Add round ears with a curved line across the top of each, and little arches for eyes. Then draw a long column that fans out into the body. At the bottom, sketch four square-shaped legs, with three in the front and one in the back.

Try Some More Speckles!

Draw nostrils spaced a little wider than the eyes. Give Speckle ossicones (the horn-like structures on giraffes' heads). Next, add a tail and a few fun spots on Speckle's back.

Shade in your giraffe, adding some more color to the spots, tail, and ossicones to make your drawing pop!

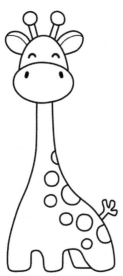

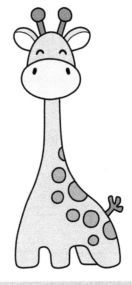

PUFFERS (THE MARSHMALLOWS)

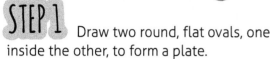

STEP 1 Draw two round, flat ovals, one inside the other, to form a plate.

STEP 2 On top of the plate, sketch three slightly misshaped circles that overlap and are stacked in the shape of a pyramid.

Practice a Couple Puffers!

STEP 3

Erase all the lines that are now covered by the two bottom marshmallows so that the top marshmallow appears behind the other two. Give the bottom marshmallows V-shaped hands. For the top marshmallow, add rounded hands resting on top of the lower marshmallows' heads.

STEP 4

Draw cute faces on each marshmallow. Give Puffers lots of character by making each marshmallow different. Draw one with an open-mouthed smile, one with big round eyes, and another with smiling eyes. Finally, make each marshmallow a different shade.

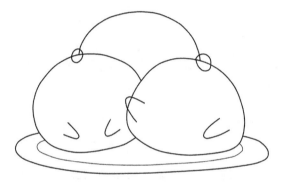

BUBBLE (THE BUNNY)

STEP 1
Draw a big circle that's slightly egg shaped.

STEP 2
Add an oval button nose and upside-down fancy V for a mouth. Draw two sideways U-shapes for arms. And a couple lumpy legs.

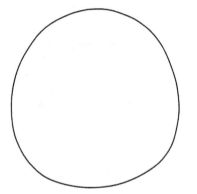

Perfect Your Bubble Skills!

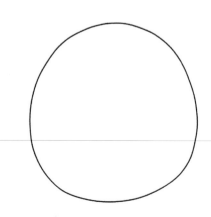

STEP 3

Give Bubble big, floppy ears (about as far apart as the arms). Sketch a smaller curve inside the bigger curve of each ear. Draw a fat carrot in Bubble's arms with three curved lines showing its shape and then a fluffy, cloud-like top.

STEP 4

Add big eyes just wider than the mouth, with small white dots in each. Shade or color in Bubble and his carrot to bring this bunny to life.

NEA (THE ICE CREAM)

STEP 1
Draw a scoop of ice cream in the shape of a fluffy cloud. Sketch the same pattern of the bottom edge underneath the first scoop.

STEP 2
Add a rectangle coming out of the top right of the ice cream. Draw round, dark eyes with a few white spots, and a V-shaped cone.

Keep Drawing More Neas!

DRAWING CHIBI

STEP 3

Erase the line behind the rectangle. Draw a crisscross pattern on the cone. Divide the rectangle on top into six even squares. Draw a simple smile between the eyes.

STEP 4

Make Nea's ice cream scoops different flavors by adding light coloring to the top scoop. Shade the cone and the rectangle and add some blush spots near the eyes to make Nea absolutely adorable!

FLURRY (THE SNOWMAN)

STEP 1
Draw a large round circle that is slightly flattened on the bottom. Underneath the circle, draw a body that gets wider toward the bottom.

STEP 2
Add a carrot-shaped nose in the lower center of the head. Sketch a scarf at the base of the neck and a droopy hat on the head.

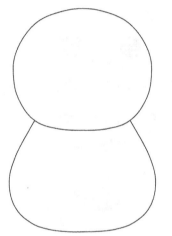

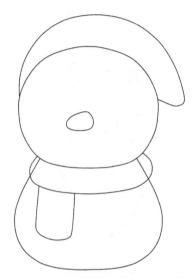

Master Your Flurry Drawing Skills!

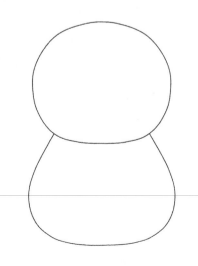

STEP 3

Erase the body lines covered by the scarf. In the center of the body, add two round buttons. Draw a ball on the end of the hat and add a fluffy edge on Flurry's forehead. Below that, add dark eyes with some white reflection spots, and a small, U-shaped smile.

STEP 4

Color in the buttons and give the scarf some fun stripes. Erase the lines of the head so the hat and its fluffy edge are seamlessly connected. Shade the hat and Flurry's carrot nose so he's finally ready for a snowball fight!

TUX (THE PENGUIN)

STEP 1

Start by drawing a large egg shape that has a flat bottom.

STEP 2

Draw short wings on either side of the body. Give Tux big, black eyes in line with the tops of the wings and leave a few white spaces in the eyes to make him even cuter. Draw small, round feet.

Bring More Tuxes to Life!

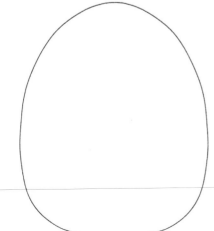

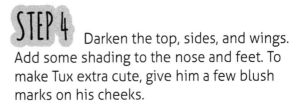

STEP 3
Erase the lines that are now covered by the feet. Draw an oval nose in between and slightly lower than the eyes. Now sketch a rounded M-shape starting where the forehead would be and extending all the way down the sides of the body.

STEP 4
Darken the top, sides, and wings. Add some shading to the nose and feet. To make Tux extra cute, give him a few blush marks on his cheeks.

GINGER (THE SUSHI)

STEP 1
To start Ginger, sketch a long, somewhat lumpy and curved oval.

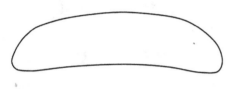

STEP 2
Underneath the oval, draw some rice that looks like a cloud. Add large, black eyes with a few white spots. On the top, draw a dollop of wasabi that looks a little like an upside-down heart.

Sharpen Your Ginger Skills!

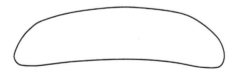

STEP 3

Erase the line covered by the wasabi. Draw some squiggly lines on the oblong piece of fish. Add a rounded W-shaped mouth.

STEP 4

Finish bringing Ginger to life by shading the wasabi and fish. Then add some supercute blush spots by the eyes!

GRILLIGAN (THE HAMBURGER)

STEP 1

Draw a rounded bun that is flat on the bottom. Give the bun a thin, squiggly skirt for lettuce.

STEP 2

Add eyes with white reflection spots, and small eyebrows. Underneath the lettuce, sketch some thin, curved shapes that connect to the lettuce above them. Make some more round and short (for the tomatoes or onions) and some longer (for the patties).

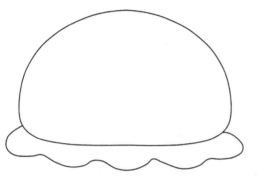

Practice the Perfect Grilligan!

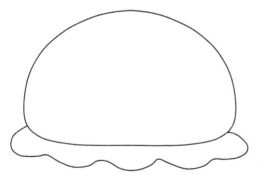

STEP 3
Draw another layer of squiggly lettuce and a rounded bun underneath. Add a cute, W-shaped mouth.

STEP 4
Lightly shade in the top and bottom buns. Leave some small white spots on top for the sesame seeds and a few spots near the eyes for blush marks. Add some darker shades to the lettuce, tomatoes, and patties.

HONEY (THE CUPCAKE)

STEP 1

Draw a bowl-like shape that is flat on the bottom, with rounded ridges at the top.

STEP 2

Add an arch that spans across the top of the cupcake wrapper. On the wrapper, draw large, round eyes with a few white spots, and small eyebrows.

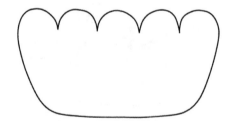

Create More Honeys!

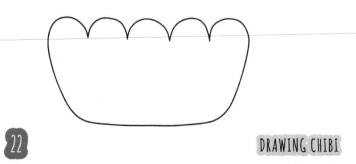

STEP 3

Draw a large swirl of icing, complete with folds and a curl on top. In between and slightly below the eyes, draw a cute, open mouth that starts in the shape of a W and extends in a long U.

STEP 4

Erase the top line of the cupcake that's covered by the icing. Shade in the cupcake and the icing, with lighter spots in the icing for sprinkles. Shade the inside of the mouth, with a lighter shade on the bottom for the tongue. Give Honey some adorable blush marks to make her extra sugar sweet!

JAWLO (THE SHARK)

STEP 1 Sketch a body that looks like a teardrop on its side.

STEP 2 Add tail fins to the pointy end of the body, and a rounded dorsal fin on top. Draw one dark, round eye with two white reflection spots in it. Right below the eye, sketch the edge of a fin hidden by the body. Then draw a larger U-shape extending out from the lower middle of the body.

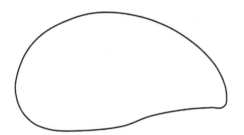

Get Jawlo Just Right!

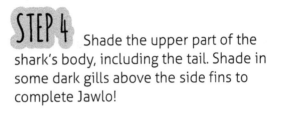

STEP 3
Erase the body lines covered up by the dorsal and side fin. Then erase the body lines so the tail fins connect smoothly. Sketch a line that separates the lower body, going under the eye and ending at the start of the tail. Add some nostrils and a mouth with sharp teeth.

STEP 4
Shade the upper part of the shark's body, including the tail. Shade in some dark gills above the side fins to complete Jawlo!

TRILL (THE PARROT)

STEP 1
Draw a round, slightly lumpy shape. The body should look similar to a bean.

STEP 2
On the left side near the center of the body, sketch an oval wing that extends just past the body. Draw two shallow, U-shaped legs. Then add a tail.

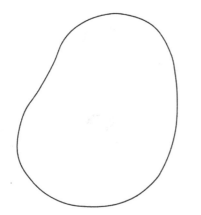

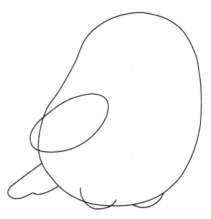

Sketch Even Better Trills!

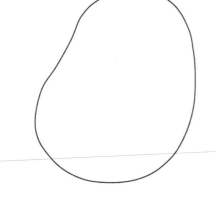

STEP 3
Erase the body lines covered by the wing and the front left leg. Give Trill some feet that look like an X and connect them to the round parts of the leg. Now sketch a beak by drawing an oval on the right edge of the parrot's head. Add a beak on top that looks like a drooping triangle and ends in a point.

STEP 4
Get rid of the right-side body line covered by the beak. Give Trill a round, white belly and shade the rest of the body. Draw a dark eye with two white spots next to the beak and add some extra color to the wing and tail to make Trill really stand out!

CEPH (THE OCTOPUS)

STEP 1 Start by sketching a round body that is slightly flat on the bottom.

STEP 2 Draw some circular eyes and shade them dark with a few white spots. Add two round tentacles to each side of the body. Draw an arch on the lower part of each tentacle and add four small suckers along the bottoms.

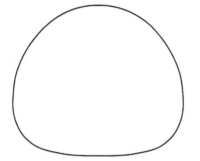

Make Some Flawless Cephs!

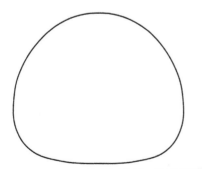

STEP 3

Draw a circle with a smaller circle inside for the mouth. Add three more round tentacles to the front of your octopus. Add the arches and suckers to the two new legs on the side, leaving the middle one blank.

STEP 4

Erase the body lines that are now covered by the tentacles. Keep the lower sections of the tentacles white while shading the suckers and the rest of Ceph's body. Make sure to keep the inside of the mouth white, too. Add some blush marks near the eyes, and Ceph is ready to go for a swim!

FIZZLE (THE FLOAT)

STEP 1 Draw a cup by sketching a rectangle that is wider at the top and becomes narrower toward the bottom.

STEP 2 Add a large dome (the lid) with a flared-out rim to the top of the rectangle. Draw some cute stick-like arms on either side and dark, round eyes with a few white reflection spots on the upper part of the cup.

Keep Drawing Fizzle!

STEP 3

Inside the lid, sketch a stack of swirling ice cream that ends slightly past the rim of the lid. Draw a straw coming out of the top of the ice cream. Then sketch a small, W-shaped mouth slightly below and in between the eyes.

STEP 4

Shade in the cup and ice cream. Add a candy-cane pattern to the straw. For some extra-cute details, highlight some blush marks and color in some dark circles near the base of the float!

GLAZE (THE DONUT)

STEP 1
Sketch a large circle.

STEP 2
Add a hole to the upper middle of the circle. Draw a dome shape on top of the circle. The dome should rise just slightly above the top of the circle, while the bottom should have a squiggly edge that ends a little below the center of the circle.

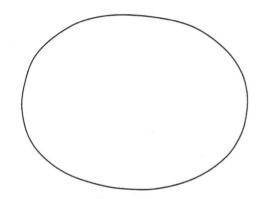

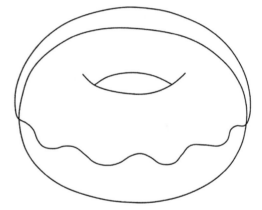

Practice a Few More Glazes!

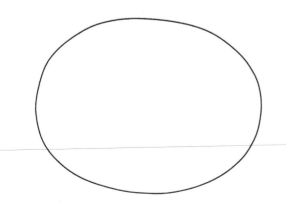

STEP 3

Erase the top line of the donut covered by the dome of icing. Draw eyes with some white reflection spots just below the donut hole. Add a mouth shaped like a rounded W.

STEP 4

Shade the icing and donut. Don't forget to add some cute, white blush marks near the eyes. Then get Glaze ready to party by coloring in some fun sprinkles all over the icing!

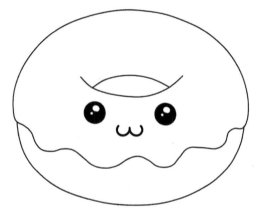

JUNIPURR (THE CAT)

STEP 1

Draw a round head that's a little flatter near the bottom. Sketch and shade in some eyes, leaving a small white dot near the top of each eye.

STEP 2

Add triangular ears with slight indents on either side of the head. Draw a tiny nose and sketch a short body that's slightly narrower at the top and fans out toward the bottom.

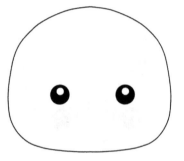

Draw the Perfect Junipurr!

STEP 3

Draw some front paws in the shape of a long U near the lower half of the body. Add small back paws on either side of the body. Then draw a small, W-shaped mouth right underneath the nose.

STEP 4

Add a tail with some stripes. Shade in some more stripes on top of the head and on the sides of the body. To complete Junipurr's look, shade in her nose and draw some whiskers on her cheeks!

HOOLIO (THE OWL)

STEP 1

For the head, draw a square-like shape that is rounded on the bottom and dips in at the top. The top corners should extend up into points. Draw a rounded body that overlaps the head.

STEP 2

Erase the top of the body covered by the head. Starting from the bottom sides of the head, draw wings that end on the middle sides of the body. Draw some cute, three-toed feet at the base of the body.

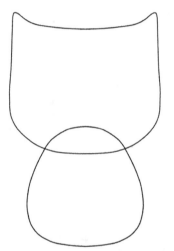

Master the Hoolio Basics!

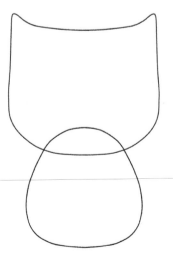

DRAWING CHIBI

STEP 3

Sketch two large, round circles that cover most of the middle and lower face but don't overlap in the middle. Sketch a small nose in between the circles. Erase the lower body lines covered by the feet.

STEP 4

Erase the lines that the nose is covering. Draw a circle on most of the body and sketch some V-shaped feathers inside. Give your owl large, dark eyes with a white dot in the center of the two face circles. Now shade in Hoolio, keeping the feet and the circles around the eyes and on the body light.

SCAMP (THE SLOTH)

STEP 1
Draw a large, circular head. Inside the head, sketch a face that dips like a heart on top and keeps close to the sides and lower edge of the head.

STEP 2
Draw thick, rounded stripes that extend from the sides of the face to almost the middle. Under the head, draw two long arms that hang down. Add a body behind these arms that extends to the right and has a small leg sticking out at the end. Draw another leg on the left side of the body.

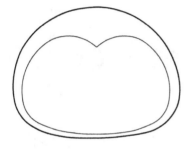

Create Even Better Scamps!

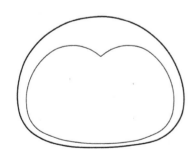

STEP 3

Add crescent-shaped eyes to the center of the two thick stripes. Then draw a small, rounded nose. On the body, outline the stomach and add three long claws to each foot.

STEP 4

Erase the body lines behind the front claws. Shade in the thick stripes and nose extra dark, keeping the eyes light. Shade in the rest of the body except the face, claws, and stomach. Now Scamp is ready to slowly cruise his way off this page!

WALLA (THE KOALA)

STEP 1
Start by drawing a rounded head and body that look like a mushroom. The head should be at least twice the size of the body.

STEP 2
Add big, round ears on either side of the head. Then add a thin ring to the outer edge of each ear. Sketch an oval near the left and right sides of the body. Then connect the top and bottom of the ovals to the body to form the feet.

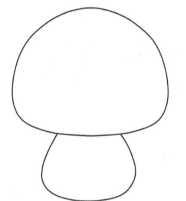

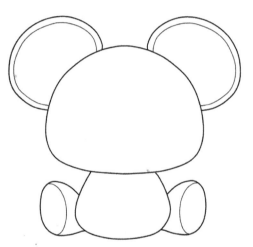

Make Walla Just Right!

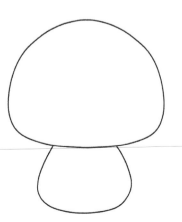

STEP 3

Draw a large, bulbous nose with a small, anchor-shaped mouth attached underneath. At the top of the body, sketch two arms that hang down just past the end of the body.

STEP 4

Erase the bottom lines of the body covered by the arms. Draw eyes with some white spots, and tiny eyebrows. Add some shading on the head, ears, and body, leaving a round section of the stomach and the bottoms of the feet unshaded. Finally, give Walla some small blush marks.

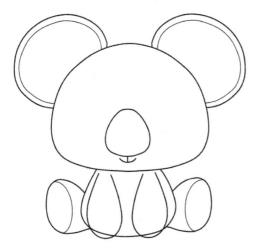 

TUGA (THE TURTLE)

STEP 1
Draw two uneven circles that overlap. The top circle should be bigger than the bottom circle.

STEP 2
Erase the line of the lower circle that's covered by the head. Color in two black eyes with small white reflections in them. On the body, draw lumpy arms and legs.

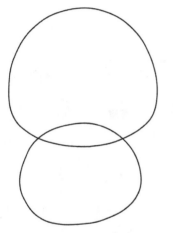

Practice Makes Perfect Tugas!

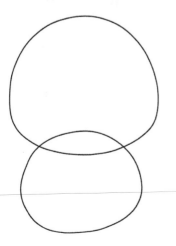

STEP 3

Give your turtle small eyebrows and an open, smiling mouth in the shape of a sideways D. Erase the lines of the body that are being covered by the left arm and leg. On the body, draw some stripes and separate the underside of the shell from the top.

STEP 4

Finish Tuga the Turtle by adding some shading! Make the underside of his shell slightly lighter than his body. Then give the top part of his shell a darker color and add some blush spots to his face.

CYMBER (THE LION)

 STEP 1 Draw a round, slightly lumpy face.

STEP 2 Add some big ears that stick out on either side of the head. Then draw a line that extends from the head in the middle of each ear. Sketch a body extending from the lower right side of the head. It should look a little like a loaf of bread. Then draw a long tail with a little tuft of hair at the end.

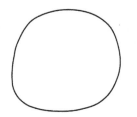

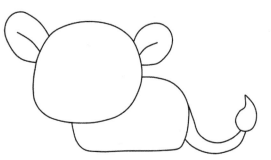

Warm Up with More Cymbers!

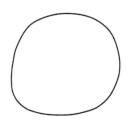

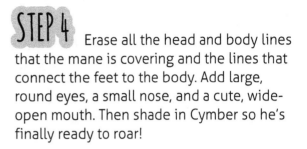

STEP 3

Now sketch a fluffy mane all around the head. The mane should cover the top and right side of the head and extend past the right ear. Make sure it also covers a good portion of the body. Then draw some shorty, stumpy legs underneath the body.

STEP 4

Erase all the head and body lines that the mane is covering and the lines that connect the feet to the body. Add large, round eyes, a small nose, and a cute, wide-open mouth. Then shade in Cymber so he's finally ready to roar!

CHOMP (THE MONKEY)

STEP 1
Draw a rounded head and body in a mushroom-like shape. Then add large eyes in the middle of the face, with small eyebrows above each eye. Make sure to leave a few white spots in the eyes.

STEP 2
Add long arms on either side of the body, just below the head. Make one arm point up and one arm point down. Sketch two circles on the bottom left and right sides of the body. Then draw a small, oblong nose between the eyes.

Keep Drawing Chomp!

STEP 3

Draw some round ears on either side of Chomp's head. Add some lips and an open, smiling mouth right under the nose. Erase the parts of the body now covered by the feet and draw a long tail that curves at the end.

STEP 4

Now shade the outer edges of the ears and head. Shade the head so that the face is heart-shaped at the top. Apply the same shading to the body, arms, legs, and tail, leaving a white circle on the stomach. To make Chomp extra cute, shade in the nose and mouth and give him a few blush spots around the eyes.

PIKA PIKA

STEP 1

Draw two lumpy circles, one on top of the other. The top circle should be slightly larger.

STEP 2

Add tall, pointed ears and a little squiggle to start the mouth. Then add short, pointed arms and legs. The left leg should overlap the body.

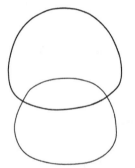

Sketch the Best Pika Pika You Can!

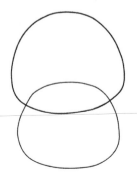

STEP 3

Erase the body line underneath the left leg. Sketch a jagged tail that overlaps the face and the right arm and ends in a chunky square. Now draw a long, open mouth just below the squiggle and give the ears black tips.

STEP 4

Finish Pika Pika's face by adding black, round eyes with white spots in them, blush marks on the cheeks, and some shading in the mouth. Erase the parts of the tail that overlap the face and right arm. Add some darker shading to the base of the tail, and Pika Pika is ready to go!

STRONG IN THE FORCE AM I

STEP 1
Draw a lumpy head that is round at the top, curves in slightly on the sides, and is flat on the bottom. Then add an uneven, rough layer underneath the head.

STEP 2
One either side of the head, sketch out a large triangle with a smaller triangle inside. Shade in some large eyes that dip toward the lower center of the face. Then draw a cape-like body that flares out at the bottom edge.

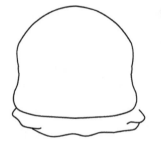

Master Your Strong Skills!

STEP 3

Add some light lines to the forehead and above the eyes. Erase a small white dot in the top middle of each eye. Then add two small nostrils and a curved smile. Draw some cloaked arms to either side of the body. Sketch more lines on the body to add texture to the cloak.

STEP 4

Now shade the cloak and the inside of the ears. Your drawing is ready to use the Force and keep order in the galaxy!

ADVANCED CHIBI ANIMALS

TUSKER (THE NARWHAL)

Sometimes people see his sharp horn and think he's dangerous, but there isn't a mean bone in Tusker's body! Tusker uses his horn to cut through icy waters, searching for his next arctic adventure. Get ready for Tusker to glide his way through these pages!

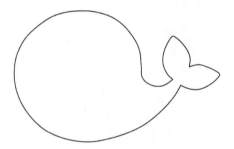

STEP 1 Start by drawing a large round body where the right side extends and curves up into a tail.

STEP 2 Sketch horizontal and vertical facial guidelines that intersect in the middle of the round part of your narwhal.

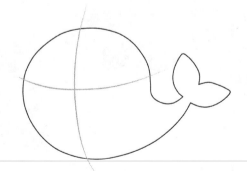

STEP 3 Draw two round, dark eyes with reflection spots along the horizontal guideline.

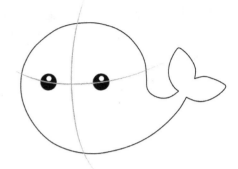

STEP 4 Directly below the center of the face, add a wavy mouth. Draw two U-shaped fins on the sides of the body.

STEP 5 Follow the vertical guideline to the very top of the head. Then move slightly to the left and sketch a spiraling horn there.

STEP 6 You may want to add some simple guidelines for the belly of the narwhal. Then erase the facial guidelines.

STEP 7 Follow your markings with a smooth, curved line to create the underside of your narwhal. Once you draw the perfect curved line for your narwhal's underbelly, erase the small guidelines you made. Then carefully erase the line of his head that is passing through the horn.

STEP 8 Time for some shading! Complete Tusker's look by adding a darker color to his upper body and leaving his stomach white. Use some light shading on his horn and around his eyes. Now, Tusker is ready to slice through some water!

Perfect Your Tusker Skills!

Practice some more Tusker drawings to get the hang of it. You can experiment with some different colors or even draw him having fun in the ocean!

Keep going from Step 1.

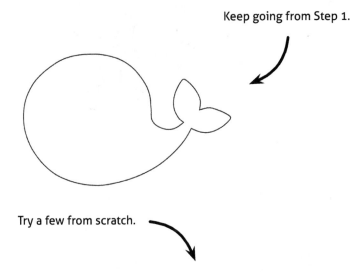

Try a few from scratch.

TRUNKO (THE ELEPHANT)

Trunko the Elephant spends his days roaming across the savanna and rolling through watering holes with his herd. But don't let his relaxed attitude fool you. Trunko loves using his strong trunk to knock down small trees, and his powerful legs are ready to stomp right off this page!

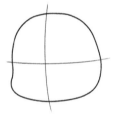

STEP 1
Draw a round head that curves in slightly on the bottom left side. Next draw horizontal and vertical facial guidelines that meet in the center of the head.

STEP 2
Add some large, flappy ears on each side of the head, with the right ear overlapping the right side of the head. Draw two small, round eyes with reflection spots on the horizontal guideline. The left eye should be a little closer to the center than the right eye. Sketch two small eyebrows above the eyes.

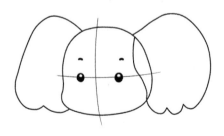

STEP 3 Erase the right side of the head that is overlapped by the ear and outline the top and sides of each ear. Draw a little tuft on top of the head. Then carefully erase the facial guidelines.

STEP 4 Connect the tuft of hair to the head. Now sketch a trunk below the eyes. The trunk should start out wide and get narrower as it flows down and curls.

STEP 5 Erase the lower face line that is now covered by the trunk. Draw a long, rounded body that looks a little bit like a bean. Make sure the body is drawn on top of most of the trunk and the lower portion of the head and ear.

STEP 6 Add four small, lumpy feet across the bottom of the body. Then erase the top lines of the body that overlap the trunk, head, and ear. Draw a curlicue tail.

STEP 7 Connect the second and fourth foot to the body. Then erase the top parts of the first and third foot that overlap with the trunk and the body. Add a few lines to the trunk and some blush spots by the eyes.

STEP 8 Shade in Trunko. Make sure the insides of his large ears are lighter than the rest of the body and darken those blush spots to get the perfect elephant!

Sketch a Few More Trunkos!

Keep drawing Trunko until you think he's perfect. Now he's ready to join his herd!

Keep going from Step 1.

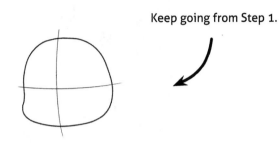

Try a few from scratch.

DIGGORY (THE DOG)

Diggory may be small, and his bark is definitely worse than his bite, but he's always ready to protect his human friends. You can count on Diggory to be loyal... and forget where he buried his bone. Maybe it's somewhere in these pages?

STEP 1
Draw a head that is slightly square-shaped, but still soft and rounded. Sketch horizontal and vertical facial guidelines that meet in the center of the head.

STEP 2
Add a nose right where the guidelines meet. Draw some triangular ears on top of the head, with smaller triangles inside each.

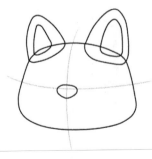

STEP 3 Erase the lines of the ears that overlap the head and add a few tufts of hair in between the ears. Add a curvy mouth beneath the nose. Then draw some lines from the bottom of the nose extending down and out to the sides of the face. Add a U-shaped chin.

STEP 4 Draw two circular eyes with reflection spots that rest right on top of the horizontal guideline. Sketch an oval-shaped body that overlaps the right bottom half of the face. Make sure to erase the small line that the chin is now covering up.

STEP 5 Now erase the upper body lines so the head is on top of the body. Draw Diggory's mouth wide open in a loud bark! Add four lumpy legs to the lower body. The third leg should be the smallest, and make the fourth leg a little wider at the top.

STEP 6 Connect the tops of the second and fourth legs to the body, and erase the tops of the first and third legs so they appear in the background of the body. Remove the facial guidelines. Then add a tall, fluffy tail and two bushy, black eyebrows.

STEP 7 Erase the small part of the tail that overlaps with the body. Then start lightly shading the nose and inside the mouth.

STEP 8 Finish your drawing with some more shading. Add darker shading to Diggory's nose, the inside of his ears, and the top of his open mouth. Add some light color to the top of the face and body. Then give your dog some cute blush spots and he's ready to get diggin'!

Keep Drawing Diggory!

Draw some more Diggorys here. Soon he'll look good enough to bark!

Keep going from Step 1.

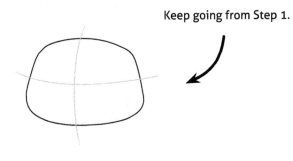

Try a few from scratch.

HOPKINS (THE RABBIT)

Hopkins doesn't go anywhere without a carrot. He uses his extra-sensitive nose to sniff out these delectable orange treats; and if you're lucky, you'll see him dig one up right on this page!

STEP 1 Draw a rounded head that has a small indent on the bottom and on the lower left side.

STEP 2 Sketch some horizontal and vertical facial guidelines that cross in the center of the head. Add two tall ears atop the head. Draw an outline inside the right ear.

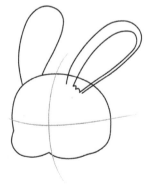

STEP 3 Erase the part of the head that is now covered by the right ear. Draw a tiny nose below the middle of the vertical guideline. Next, sketch out a round half-circle starting at the bottom right edge of the head. Next to this half-circle, add an open curve.

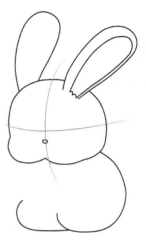

STEP 4 On the horizontal guideline draw two dark, round eyes with reflection spots, and tiny eyebrows above them. Connect the left side of the body to the head by drawing a small arm. Add another arm near the center of the body.

STEP 5 Erase the facial guidelines. Sketch two small feet on the bottom edge of the body. Add a circle for a tail to the right side of the body.

STEP 6 Erase the tops of the feet and the left side of the tail that overlap the body. Draw a small carrot between your rabbit's two hands.

STEP 7 Make the carrot appear as if Hopkins is holding it close by erasing the parts of the carrot that the hands overlap.

STEP 8 Now add some light shading to the inside of Hopkins ear and two blush spots by his eyes. Then give the carrot some color, and Hopkins is ready to nibble on his little snack!

Warm Up with More Hopkins!

Keep practicing your Hopkins sketches until you think you've got the hang of it!

Keep going from Step 1.

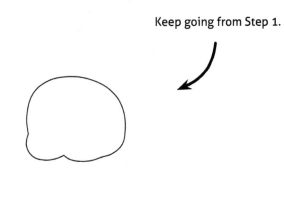

Try a few from scratch.

KITLYN (THE CAT)

Kitlyn loves to preen and be pampered as much as the next cat, but don't let her fool you into thinking she's a total diva. When you're not looking, Kitlyn might try to catch a few mice or claw her way right off this page!

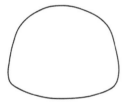

STEP 1 Start by drawing a round head that is a little flatter on the bottom.

STEP 2 Draw horizontal and vertical facial guidelines that meet in the center of the head. Add some triangular ears on top of the head. Now draw a curved line facing outward in each ear.

STEP 3 Erase the lines of the head covered by the ears and the bottom of the ears so they connect seamlessly with the head. On the horizontal guideline, draw two large circles for eyes, with small arched eyebrows above.

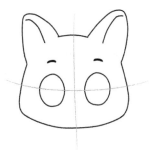

STEP 4 Add some tufts of fur to the base of the ears and by the cheeks. Draw a dark half-circle with a few lashes around the top and sides of each eye. Add a small nose in the center, level with the bottom of the eyes. Sketch a body that widens as you reach the base. Then draw a circle inside most of the body.

STEP 5 Draw a small W underneath the nose. Then sketch two long legs starting at the top of the body and extending all the way to the bottom. Make them curve toward each other, and then erase the body lines that they are now covering.

STEP 6

Draw a small open mouth under the W. Then sketch out two oval feet that slightly overlap the base of the body and the legs. Carefully erase the facial guidelines.

STEP 7

Erase the tops of the feet covering the body and legs. Add a tall, fluffy tail and shade the end darker than the rest. Continue to add light shading with some darker stripes to the rest of your cat, except the stomach. For the eyes, shade in an iris with a darker pupil.

STEP 8

Now go back and darken up some of your shading to make Kitlyn really stand out!

Practice More Kitlyns!

Don't be afraid to practice drawing Kitlyn until you get her just right. She loves all the attention!

Keep going from Step 1.

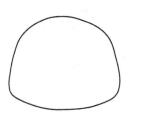

Try a few from scratch.

PIERCE (THE UNICORN)

Pierce may have a giant and very sharp horn, but he never uses it for evil. Most days, you can find this unicorn using his horn to get those hard-to-reach items off the top shelf or poking through the apple trees for his next meal. But be vigilant. Mythical creatures like Pierce tend to disappear right off the page!

STEP 1 Draw an oval-shaped head that gets flatter on the lower right side. Sketch horizontal and vertical facial guidelines that meet slightly lower than the middle of the face.

STEP 2 Draw a spiraled horn coming out from the forehead. Add two round, black eyes on the horizontal guideline. Then erase a white spot in each eye.

STEP 3 Erase the top of the head that's covered by the horn. Now sketch a flowing mane surrounding the horn and running down the right side of the head. Add two small eyebrows and some nostrils on the lower part of the face.

STEP 4 Draw a smile that curves up off the end of the face and ends close to the right nostril. Erase all the lines of the head that are now covered by the mane.

STEP 5 Draw two long legs. The left one should start out touching the head but the other end stops just short. The second leg should be under the mane. You can now carefully erase the facial guidelines.

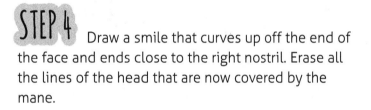

STEP 6

Draw ovals next to and overlapping both legs. Then draw a line through the bottom of the legs that connects these two circles. Now sketch the rest of the body coming out from beneath Pierce's mane.

STEP 7

Erase the lines that overlap the two front legs. Give your unicorn a long, sweeping tail.

STEP 8

Draw an arch across the face and above the nostrils. Then complete your unicorn drawing by adding some fun shading! Give Pierce some dark hooves and a rainbow tail and mane. Add some blush spots to make this unicorn extra adorable!

DRAWING CHIBI

Keep Sketching Pierce!

Draw Pierce as many times as you can before he decides to gallop off this page!

Keep going from Step 1.

Try a few from scratch.

CHICXULUB (THE DINOSAUR)

Chicxulub, named after the meteor that is said to have wiped out the dinosaurs, is more cheerful than his namesake. Although his sharp teeth and long claws seem scary, Chicxulub only wants to spend his days stomping in mud and chasing butterflies!

STEP 1
Stat by drawing a lumpy head that almost looks like a misshapen, rounded diamond. Make sure the bottom right of the head ends in a prominent point.

STEP 2
Near the top left of the head, draw a small line and then draw a circle coming out of it. Sketch an arch above this circle. Now draw a small bump coming out of the other side of the head.

STEP 3 Erase the lines now covered by the circle and arch. To turn this circle into an eye, shade it in almost completely, leaving only a white edge on the right side. Next, add a giant nose extending out of the forehead and coming back right under the eye. Draw an open mouth under the nose.

STEP 4 Erase the line of the face that the nose is covering. Then add a small white circle in the eye.

STEP 5 Next, draw a U-shaped body that is thicker in the middle and gets narrow toward the tail. Give your dinosaur's back a few shallow ridges.

STEP 6
Now sketch the legs. Start by drawing a large open-ended circle on the lower body. Underneath this circle, draw a leg and foot that has three toes with sharp claws. Sketch a small bump on the lower right side of the body and draw another leg and foot.

STEP 7
Erase the line of the lower body that the left thigh is covering up. Then draw two small arms that end in some more sharp claws. On the face, give your dinosaur's mouth rows of pointy teeth and draw two big nostrils on the nose.

STEP 8
Chicxulub is ready for some shading! Add some light color to his entire body and use a darker shade inside the mouth. Then, to make him even more spectacular, play around with shading some patterns on his body and face.

Create Even Better Chicxulubs!

Don't stop at just one. Practice your skills until the perfect Chicxulub comes to life and is ready to dodge some meteors!

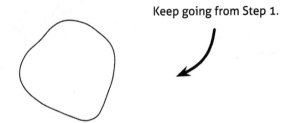

Keep going from Step 1.

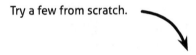

Try a few from scratch.

DORAGON (THE DRAGON)

This little dragon might not look like the scariest creature in the castle...but adorable looks can be deceiving. That little tail can break walls, those small wings can take to the sky, and inside that snout is a whole lot of smoke and fire ready to burn up this page!

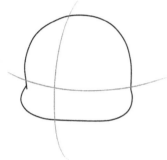

STEP 1
Draw a lumpy head that is more round at the top and flat on the bottom, with a little indent on the bottom left side. Then sketch horizontal and vertical facial guidelines. These two lines should meet a little to the left of the center of the head.

STEP 2
Add a horn to the middle of your dragon's forehead and two more on either side of the head. Draw more horns going down the back, each horn a little smaller than the last. Next add a snout with nostrils on the lower half of Doragon's face.

STEP 3

Erase the lower face line that the snout is now covering. Add round eyes that are centered on the horizontal guideline. Make the left eye slightly smaller and more oblong than the right. Sketch tiny eyebrows above the eyes. Now draw a bean-shaped body, with the right side curling up in the middle so it almost forms a circle. Add a small foot at the base of this circle.

STEP 4

Add a long, sweeping tail. Draw a thin L-shape for a leg down the left side of the body. Sketch another rounded leg over the existing right foot and thigh. Make sure this leg goes slightly past where the body ends and is level with the other foot.

STEP 5

Carefully erase your facial guidelines. Then erase the top and right side of the new leg so that the right foot and thigh are once again uncovered. Give your little dragon unfurled wings and draw some fringe along the outside edge and at the end of the tail.

STEP 6
Now comes the fun part: adding detail! Outline the inside edges of the wings and add some lines to make the wings look sinewy. On the three feet, draw rounded claws.

STEP 7
Fill in the eyes, leaving a small white circle at the top. Erase the lines of the feet that are covered by claws. Be careful not to erase any of your claws!

STEP 8
To really make this adorable dragon fly off the page, add some shading. Make the horns, claws, tail fringe, and the outline of the wings slightly darker. Finally, darken the eyes even further. Doragon is now ready to take flight and breathe fire!

Draw a Few More Doragons!

Perfect your skills at drawing Doragon until he's the best he can be! If you want, you can even make him breathe fire or give him a pile of gold to guard.

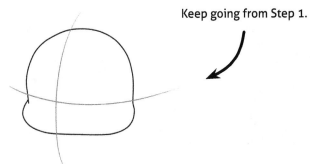

Keep going from Step 1.

Try a few from scratch.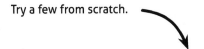

BODY

Drawing a body isn't the easiest thing in the world, but it's important to learn the basics. Get ready to perfect your body-drawing skills so you can master all the fun, diverse Chibi people in the next part of this book!

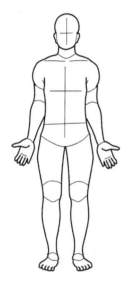

STEP 1 It can be helpful when drawing Chibi bodies to think about it as simply changing the size and dimension of real-life body parts. Typically when drawing Chibi, the head, legs, and torso each make up ⅓ of the body. In this section, we're going to go step-by-step through how to shrink an adult human into an adorable Chibi character!

STEP 2 First, start by enlarging the head and softening and simplifying the shape of the limbs. On a realistic human body, the head makes up only ⅛ of the entire body. In this step, we're doubling the size so it makes up ¼ of the body.

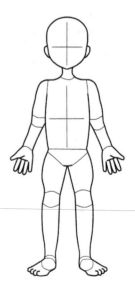

DRAWING CHIBI

STEP 3 Now take a look at what happens when we increase the size of the head so that it makes up ⅓ of the body! The proportions are becoming very exaggerated.

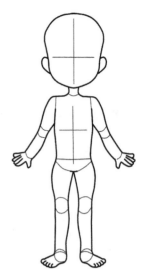

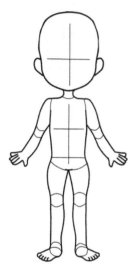

STEP 4 On a realistic human head, the top of the head (from the forehead up) is actually wider and taller than you might think—it takes up about ½ of the entire head. In this step, we shrunk it a bit.

STEP 5 Now begin to really soften the body. Instead of having complex contours around the shoulders, torso, and legs, each part of the body on our Chibi character is made up of simple, rounded, oval-like shapes

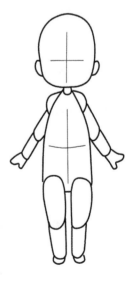

STEP 6

Here's the real trick...we need to keep inflating that Chibi character head, almost like it's a balloon. Start blowing it up!

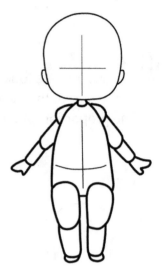

STEP 7

Thought we couldn't get any bigger? Ha, think again! Keep making that head wider, taller, and bigger!

STEP 8

We've gone from a realistic human form, where the head made up just $\frac{1}{8}$ of the body, to this! In our final step of this transformation, we've created a Chibi character with a head that takes up a full half of the whole body!

Get the Hang of Chibi Bodies!

Use the space below to draw more Chibi bodies. Play around with different head, arm, body, and leg sizes until you feel like you've drawn the perfect Chibi body!

Start with a realistic human body,

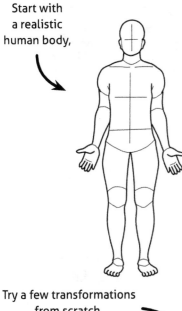

and transform it into an adorable Chibi character.

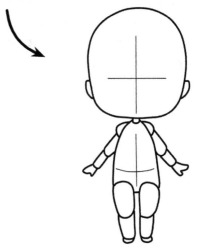

Try a few transformations from scratch.

FACE

Faces come in all shapes and sizes, so learning the fundamentals of drawing a face will help when you want to draw all kinds of faces in the future. Whether you're drawing a long face, a square face, or a cat's face, after this section, you'll be ready to flawlessly sketch anything with two eyes, a nose, and a mouth!

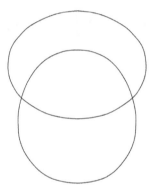

STEP 1

When beginning a face, it's easier to draw some shapes you're already familiar with rather than attempting a specific face shape right off the bat. So to start, sketch a large round circle that is slightly egg shaped. Then draw a large oval on top of your circle.

STEP 2

Now add some horizontal and vertical guidelines. These lines should meet just below the bottom of the oval.

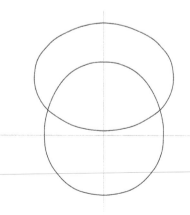

STEP 3 Now sketch the outline of a face using the edges of your circle and oval as a guide. Your face should indent on the sides of the circle and come to a rounded point at the bottom.

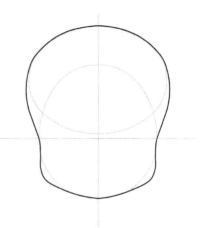

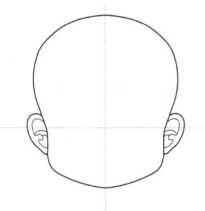

STEP 4 Erase your oval and circle guides, but make sure to leave the facial guidelines. Then draw ears in the indents of the face. Use the horizontal guideline to center your ears and keep them even on both sides.

STEP 5 Draw two large, round eyes. The middle of each eye should rest on the horizontal guideline and each eye should be an equal distance from the vertical guideline. Next sketch a tiny V-shaped nose on the vertical guideline and a small smile below the nose.

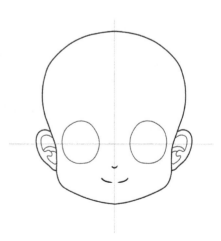

STEP 6 Add some thick eyelashes above each eye and some small, dark eyebrows higher up on the forehead.

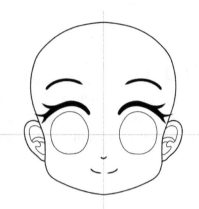

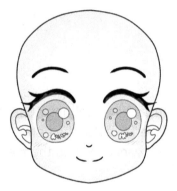

STEP 7 Carefully erase the facial guidelines. Now add some details inside the eyes. Add some pupils, some light shading, and some reflection spots.

STEP 8 Darken the pupils and irises of the eyes, and make some of the reflection spots brighter. Then give the face more dimension by lightly shading around the edges.

Become a Face Expert!

Repetition is key to being able to draw great faces! Use your oval and circle guidelines to experiment with different face shapes, eye sizes, and more!

Keep going from Step 1.

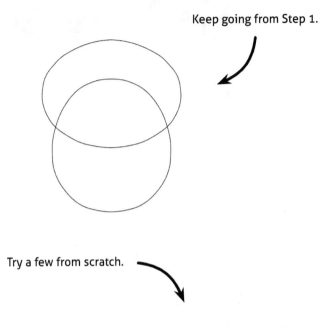

Try a few from scratch.

EYES

A major part of any character you draw is the eyes. Eyes can often show the emotions a creature or person is feeling better than a smile or frown can. Narrowed eyes might convey anger while wide-open and shining eyes could mean surprise. One of the best ways to give your drawing character is by mastering the basics of eyes!

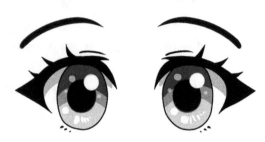

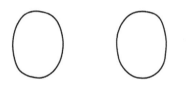

STEP 1
To start your basic eye drawing, sketch two round, slightly oval circles.

STEP 2
Add some light shading to the circles. Starting on the outer sides of each eye, draw a pointed triangle shape that then curves up, around, and comes to rest on the top of each eye, with the end starting to point down the inside of each eye. Now shade in the structure.

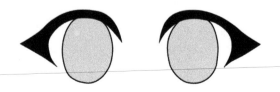

STEP 3 Next, draw round pupils in the center of each eye. On the edges of the dark outline of the eyes, add some lashes.

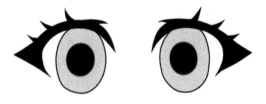

STEP 4 To give your eyes some more small details, draw a flat line above the lashes closer to the top of the eyes. Then add a few tiny dots around the lower edge of each eye. Inside each eye, make the upper half of the pupil slightly darker.

STEP 5 Sketch dark eyebrows above each eye that arch downward. Finish shading the eyes by coloring the top third of the pupils even darker.

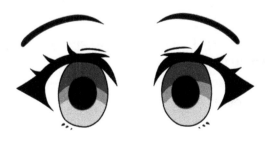

STEP 6 Adding reflection spots to any eyes will make them look more realistic. For these eyes, make a bright white spot on the top right side of each pupil and a smaller, slightly less bright reflection spot near the bottom left of the pupil.

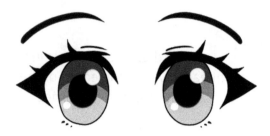

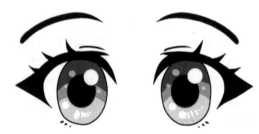

STEP 7 Keep adding varying reflection spots around the pupil until you're happy with the way your eyes look.

STEP 8 As a last touch to give your eyes some more dimension, lightly shade the top of the space between the dark eyelashes and the eyes.

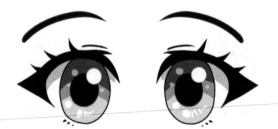

DRAWING CHIBI

Practice Makes Perfect Eyes!

Use the templates below to hone your eye-drawing skills. Practice eyes with thick eyebrows, eyes with small lashes, eyes that are squinting, and eyes wide with shock. The possibilities are endless!

Keep going from Step 1.

Try a few from scratch.

HAIR

Hair is another important element when drawing characters, especially humans. Hair can tell you a lot about someone's style and personality. Whether you want to draw a character with long, flowing hair, a mohawk, or a braided updo, learning how to sketch the fundamental shapes and lines of hair will bring to life any number of creatures you put on these pages!

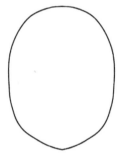

STEP 1 The best way to begin drawing hair is by first drawing the head you want your character to have. For the hair in this section, start by drawing a round head.

STEP 2 Cover the forehead with a mixture of long and short sections of hair that remain connected. These sections can curl around the edges, hang straight down, or stick to the sides of the face.

STEP 3 Draw two more sections of hair surrounding the left side of the head. Make these strands of hair slightly longer than the hair on the forehead, and make the ends point outward and curve upward.

STEP 4 Repeat a similar pattern of hair on the right side of the head.

STEP 5 Now connect the two sides of hair in an arc over the top of the head. Where the two sides meet in the middle, add a small wisp of hair.

STEP 6 Draw longer strands of hair coming out of the bottom of the hair on the left side of the head. Give this hair thick and thin sections, with the ends curling slightly. Make the hair stop short of the chin.

STEP 7 Sketch the same hair on the opposite side of the head. Try to give this section of hair the same type of strands and the same slightly curled ends. Then erase the lines of the head that are now covered by hair.

STEP 8 To finish your hair, add lots of shades. Shade the top of the head, around the edges, and the underside of the hair a darker color. Add some lighter shading to the rest with some very light or white streaks throughout.

Become a Hair Master!

Draw some more hairstyles below. Make your hair even longer or shorter. Add some braids or corkscrew curls. Whatever you decide, don't forget to add shading to make your hair three-dimensional!

Keep going from Step 1.

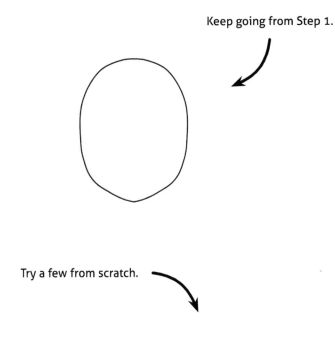

Try a few from scratch.

ADVANCED
CHIBI PEOPLE

WUBBA (THE BABY)

Wubba may not be able to do most things that adults can, but he still knows how to have fun. Watch him as he uses his small arms and legs to crawl his way to new adventures filled with milk, bottles, and the occasional sweet treat!

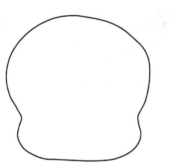

STEP 1
Draw a large, lumpy head that looks a little like an upside-down and rounded piece of sliced bread.

STEP 2
Sketch a vertical guideline straight down the middle of the head. The horizontal guideline should rest just above the indents in the sides of the head. At the top center of the head, draw a curling lock of hair. In the indents on each side, draw rounded ears.

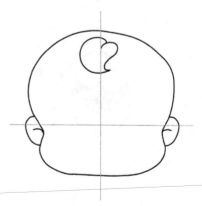

STEP 3 Add two large, round eyes with the centers resting on the horizontal guideline. Draw a line across the top, inside edge of the head. Make sure this line doesn't go through the little tuft of hair.

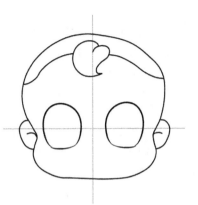

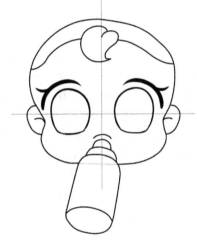

STEP 4 Above each eye, draw some dark arches that curve slightly down the sides of the eyes. Add a small eyelash at the lower-middle of each arch. Below the eyes on the vertical guideline, draw a small arch. Directly underneath that arch, sketch a bottle.

STEP 5 Draw two eyebrows above the eyelashes. Then draw two chubby arms and hands starting from the bottom of the face and curving around the bottle.

STEP 6 Erase the facial guidelines carefully. Then draw a rounded foot with small circular toes underneath the right arm. Then draw small bits of the body by sketching two squiggly lines from the left side of the foot to the bottle. Finish this side of the body by drawing a tiny line from the bottom left edge of the foot to the closest squiggly line. This is the leg.

STEP 7 Draw another big foot on the left side of the body. Once again connect the bottom edge of this foot to the bottle with a tiny line. In the small space between the foot, bottle, and bottom edge of the arm, draw another tiny line connecting the foot and the bottle. Then start giving your eyes more detail by adding a pupil and some reflection spots. Give your baby's hair, the contents of the bottle, and the lower part of the body some light shading.

STEP 8 Make the pupils even darker and some of the reflection spots in the eyes even lighter. Give the irises of each eye varying shades of color, making the bottom the lightest and the top the darkest. Shade the lower part of the body and the bottle darker. Finish your baby by giving him some adorable blush spots and shading between the eyes and eyelashes.

Keep Drawing Wubba!

Use the space below to get the hang of drawing adorable babies. Wubba will only get cuter the more you practice drawing him!

Keep going from Step 1.

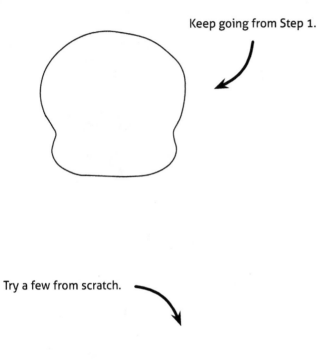

Try a few from scratch.

SILAS (THE ELDERLY MAN)

Silas likes to spend his days of retirement living a quiet life...or does he? Rumor has it this friendly old man is a top-secret spy that spends his nights traveling to foreign countries and gathering intelligence. While you'll often find Silas sitting in the park feeding the birds during the day, don't forget he's always ready to spring into action at a moment's notice!

STEP 1 Draw a large head that's rounded at the top and flatter on the bottom. Give the face two slight indents on the lower sides.

STEP 2 Sketch horizontal and vertical facial guidelines that meet in the center of the head.

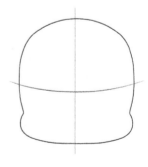

STEP 3 Draw two round eyes with small reflection spots in each on the horizontal guideline. They should be the same distance away from the vertical line. Then add a body underneath the head that gets slightly wider toward the bottom.

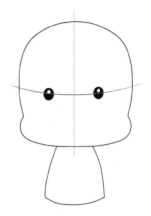

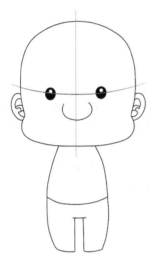

STEP 4 On the sides of the head underneath the horizontal guideline, draw two small ears. Add a bulbous nose below the eyes. Then sketch some pants with rectangular legs at the bottom of the body.

STEP 5 Directly below the nose, add an open, U-shaped mouth with two small teeth. Draw a few wrinkle lines on the forehead and cheeks. Then draw some arms coming out of the upper sides of the body. Make the left arm bent and waving. Then sketch two feet coming out of the pant legs.

STEP 6 Now add some tufts of hair on the sides of the head, bushy eyebrows, and a mustache on both sides of the nose. Then erase the small face line under the left hand.

STEP 7 Erase the facial guidelines carefully. Now add some more detail to Silas's clothes. Give his shirt a V-neck, a pocket, and a striped edge. Draw the sleeves halfway down the arms. Draw some pockets on the pants and cut the shoes off at the ankle.

STEP 8 Finish drawing Silas by adding some shading. Lightly color his shirt. Use a darker shade on his pants and an even darker shade for his shoes.

DRAWING CHIBI

Bring More Silases to Life!

Practice drawing Silas until you think you've got him just right. You can even try drawing him with some of the gear he uses on his secret missions!

Keep going from Step 1.

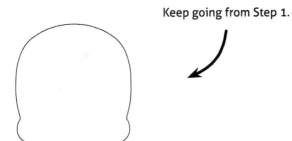

Try a few from scratch.

HIYAH (THE NINJA)

Growing up, Hiyah always wanted to be a ninja. Just because he's small doesn't mean he isn't the fiercest ninja ever trained. Hiyah's small stature let's him easily sneak past his enemies and use his strong arms to toss his throwing star right off this page!

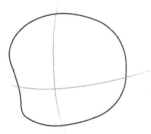

STEP 1 Draw a rounded face with a gradual indent along the left side. This face shape is popular throughout this book. Add horizontal and vertical facial guidelines that meet in the lower middle of the head.

STEP 2 Draw two round, slightly lumpy eyes along the horizontal guideline. The left eye should be very close to the outer edge of the face. Add dark eyebrows directly above each eye. Now sketch a long, slightly bent body.

STEP 3
On the top right side of the body, draw an arm pointing straight out. Add a small, mitten-like hand. Draw the left arm as if it's pointing at you. Start with a small lump coming out of the upper left side of the body. Then draw another round lump over the first one and slightly to the right. Finally, draw a fisted hand on the right side of the second lump.

STEP 4
Erase the body line the left arm is now covering. Draw the right leg pointing straight out and a little to the right. Draw the left leg drawn up and bent at the knee. The top part of the left thigh should overlap the body. Add small rounded feet to each leg.

STEP 5
Draw a hood that covers the top part of the head and ends in a point. Then draw a line between the sides of the hood and across the top of the eyebrows. Sketch a mask that covers the lower face, with the two sides coming to a point where the facial guidelines meet. Now erase the small line where the left thigh overlaps the leg.

STEP 6 Carefully erase the facial guidelines. Then erase the lines of the head that are covered by the hood. Now it's time to add lots of detail. Draw a throwing star in Hiyah's right hand, add patterned cuffs to each sleeve, draw a crisscrossed belt around his chest and waist, and add a small knife to the right side of the body. Finally, add another layer of clothing over the top part of the legs.

STEP 7 Erase the lines of the top parts of the legs that are now covered up. Also erase the small line of the body that the handle of the knife is overlapping.

STEP 8 Give your ninja's eyes an iris and a pupil. Finally, to make Hiyah look like the most dangerous ninja, add some shading. Apply light shading to his clothes and darker shading to his pants, sleeves, belt, and throwing star.

Sharpen Your Hiyah!

Draw Hiyah the ninja until he's as sharp as can be! Once you've got the basics down, he'll be ready to jump into any action-packed adventure you throw his way!

Keep going from Step 1.

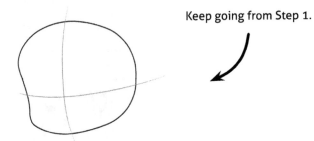

Try a few from scratch.

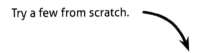

BRAYN (THE ZOMBIE)

Brayn isn't like other zombies. He goes to school during the day and likes hanging out with friends on the weekends. However, his favorite food is...you guessed it, brains. But despite his odd hankering for a brain or two, Brayn the Zombie is just like you!

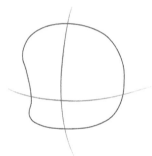

STEP 1
Draw a rounded face with a slight indent along the left side. Add horizontal and vertical facial guidelines that meet in the lower middle of the head.

STEP 2
Beneath the horizontal guideline, draw ears that stick out on either side of the head. Sketch two eyes that look like half-circles. The bottom of the eyes should rest on the horizontal guideline. Now add a rectangular body.

STEP 3

Add some crazy hair that sticks out from the top of the head. Draw some flowing strands of hair along the forehead. Above each eye, sketch two small, chunky eyebrows. Then erase the line separating the head from the right ear so it's fully connected.

STEP 4

Erase the line of the head separating the bangs from the rest of the hair. Draw a long, oval-shaped mouth with two rows of uneven teeth.

STEP 5

Draw two arms that are bent at the elbows with the ends pointing upward. Then add two legs slightly bent at the knees.

STEP 6

Sketch hands and feet. Give the hands that claw-like shape that is a classic zombie pose. Add a tiny nose where the two guidelines meet.

STEP 7

Erase the facial guidelines and the small lines of the arms where the hands overlap. Draw tattered shorts over the legs, and add a line on each upper arm to make a shirt. Sketch a few tears and stains on the shorts and shirt.

STEP 8

Remove the lines of the legs that the shorts are covering. Now complete your zombie by adding some shading to his hair and clothes.

Practice Brayn!

Get this zombie ready to search for his next brain meal by developing your Brayn the Zombie drawing skills!

Keep going from Step 1.

Try a few from scratch.

POLARIA (BEAR ONESIE)

Polaria's favorite animals are bears, from polar to grizzly to brown. Watch as she puts on her bear onesie and becomes just as strong and powerful as any bear right on this page!

STEP 1 Start by sketching a lumpy head that has a small indent along the left side.

STEP 2 Draw horizontal and vertical facial guidelines that meet in the center of the head. Then add a hood that surrounds the top and sides of the head.

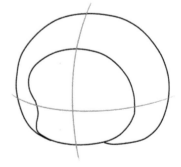

STEP 3 Atop the hood, draw two small half-circle ears. Sketch two large, round eyes centered on the horizontal guideline. Then, draw a U-shaped, open mouth on the vertical guideline. Add an oval-shaped body.

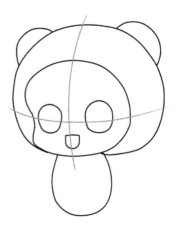

STEP 4 Draw some dark eyebrows and eyelashes above the eyes. Then add some long and slightly chunky arms and legs. The left arm should be raised up near the face.

STEP 5 Erase the top lines of the legs and the left arm that overlap the body. Then erase all the lines inside the right arm so that this arm rests on top. Now carefully erase the facial guidelines. Add two small, round eyes and an adorably tiny nose to the top of the hood. Then give your character two hands and two rounded feet.

STEP 6
Remove the top lines of the feet that overlap the legs. Now put those hair skills you learned earlier to use. Give Polaria long, flowing hair that reaches down to her arms.

STEP 7
Erase the hair lines that overlap with the left hand and arm. Then erase the bottom right line of the hood that is now covered by hair. Start some light shading. Shade the arms, legs, feet, and the ears of the hood. Then give some color to her hair and shade in the mouth. Now add some light detail to the eyes.

STEP 8
Complete Polaria by adding more color! Darken the pupils of the eyes an add some more shading to the irises. Then give more color to the arms, legs, and ears on the onesie.

Get Polaria Just Right

Make Polaria the most powerful she can be by developing your bear onesie drawing skills in the space below.

Keep going from Step 1.

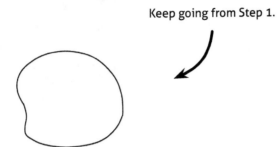

Try a few from scratch.

VIXEN (FOX ONESIE)

Vixen is ready for fun and adventure, and she never goes anywhere without her fox suit. Dressed as a fox, she can run as fast and is just as clever as those cute, orange and white creatures. Now, she's ready to begin an adventure right on this page!

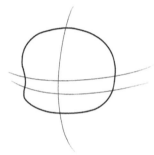

STEP 1
Draw a circular shape with the left side indented slightly. Sketch one vertical and two horizontal guidelines that meet near the center of the face.

STEP 2
Draw circular eyes that rest on the lower horizontal guideline. The left eye should also be closer to the vertical guideline than the right eye. Add wavy hair around the face that stretches past the chin. Frame the face with some bangs.

STEP 3   Add very dark lashes and eyebrows above the eyes. Draw a bigger U-shape around the top of the head to start the fox hood.

STEP 4   Erase the top of the head that is now covered by the hood and add on some triangle-shaped ears. Draw a slight, curved smile and a tiny nose where the vertical and the lower horizontal guidelines meet. Next, make a cylinder-like body and draw an oval in the middle-lower section.

STEP 5   Sketch some arms and legs, with the left arm bent inward. These limbs should slightly overlap the body. Color in two round, dark eyes on the fox hood. Give the fox a nose.

STEP 6 Remove the lines of the arms and legs that overlap the body. Then erase the facial guidelines without removing the little nose.

STEP 7 Outline the inner edge of the fox hood and dip down in the middle to meet the nose. Add some chunky feet and a more-detailed right hand to Vixen's body. Draw a tiny circle for the left hand. Add some light shading to the eyes, hair, fox hood, body, and limbs.

STEP 8 Erase the lines of the feet that overlap the legs. Do the same for the small hand that overlaps part of the arm and body so only a small bump is visible. Add dark round pupils to the center of the eyes while lightening parts of the iris. For some finishing details, darken the hair and the fox nose.

Sharpen Your Vixen Skills!

Practice some more Vixen drawings to get the hang of it. You can even switch things up by adding some color or drawing a different hairstyle. The fun never stops with Vixen!

Keep going from Step 1.

Try a few from scratch.

CERA (DINO ONESIE)

Don't let the fluffy hood and soft material fool you. This dinosaur's tail can smash through anything and its teeth are as sharp as can be. Get ready for Cera to bring some prehistoric charm right to this page!

STEP 1
First draw a rounded head. Then draw a layer surrounding part of the head, starting from the top left and extending all the way down to the bottom right side. This is going to be the hood of the onesie.

STEP 2
Sketch horizontal and vertical facial guidelines that meet in the lower middle of the head. Add another thin layer on top of the one you already drew. This layer should stop halfway down the right side of the head and remain open-ended. Draw a third layer that's thicker and extends down the right side of the head and connects to the bottom right side. Then add two tiny nostrils to the top of the second layer.

STEP 3 Draw two round, black eyes on the third layer above each nostril. Sketch some hair across the forehead and down the right side of the face.

STEP 4 Add more hair falling down the left side of the face. Draw one round eye that rests on the horizontal guideline and has dark eyelashes and a thin dark eyebrow above it. To the hood, add some pointy teeth across the top of the first layer. On the outer edge of the hood, draw some spikes going down the dino's head. Finally, give your character a small oblong body with a line down the center.

STEP 5 Draw a second eye with eyelashes and an eyebrow. Now sketch an edge around both sides of the body that extends down and forms into two legs.

STEP 6

Add short arms, two small feet, and a thick, pointed tail to your dino onesie. Start giving the eyes a few details.

STEP 7

Now draw a tiny nose, an upward curved smile, and add two hands to the body. Then carefully erase the facial guidelines. Add more spikes going down the dino tail.

STEP 8

Fill out some final details to make Cera come to life! Darken the pupils and shade the irises of the eyes. Then add some dark shading to the dino onesie and even darker shading to the shoes.

Create More Ceras!

Improve your dino drawing skills and practice making Cera as cute and intimidating as you can. Get it just right and Cera will be ready to roar!

Keep going from Step 1.

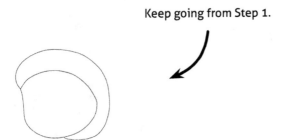

Try a few from scratch.

VIGIL (THE SUPERHERO)

With his small body and his ability to fly, Vigil was born to be a fast-paced, action-packed superhero. And while he hasn't found the perfect superhero name yet, Vigil doesn't let that stop him from going out and saving the day when there are people who need help!

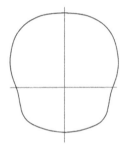

STEP 1
Start by making a rounded head that narrows slightly toward the bottom. Draw horizontal and vertical facial guidelines that meet a little below the center of the head.

STEP 2
Draw an eye mask across the face. Use the guidelines to keep the mask even on both sides. The eyes should rest on the horizontal guideline.

STEP 3

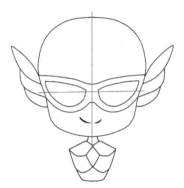

Add a small smile below the mask. Then draw a tiny neck with a small pentagon-shaped body underneath it. Sketch some shapes across the body. Add a wing-like structure to each side of the head.

STEP 4

Draw an arch around the top of the head. Sketch a diamond in the center of the forehead. Add straps to the sides of the diamond that stretch to the outer edges of the head. Carefully erase the facial guidelines. Now draw a skirt-like piece of clothing underneath the body. The front of this skirt should be open.

STEP 5

Erase the inner line of the top of the head. Then draw two arms. Give the arms extra detail like shoulder pads and elbow pads.

STEP 6

Now sketch two legs coming out of the skirt-like piece of clothing. Give the legs small knee pads.

STEP 7

Go through and erase any small lines that have been overlapped by other parts. Then draw two square-like feet.

STEP 8

Finally, add some shading. Make the eye mask and parts of the arms and legs extra dark. Then lightly shade in parts of the helmet and body suit until Vigil is ready to go out and save the day!

Draw the Perfect Vigil!

If you practice Vigil until he's perfect, he'll be ready to keep crime off the streets and save his city from any and every villain out there.

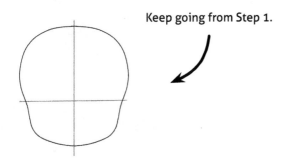

Keep going from Step 1.

Try a few from scratch.

MARINA (THE MERMAID)

Marina spends her long summer days sunning herself on the rocks of her favorite cove and collecting gorgeous seashells to add to her necklace. Watch as this mermaid comes to life ready to dive right off this page!

STEP 1
Draw a rounded head with a shallow indent on the left side. Then sketch horizontal and vertical facial guidelines that meet near the center of the face. Then add a second horizontal guideline underneath the first.

STEP 2
Draw large, round eyes that rest on the lower horizontal guideline. Draw a body with a narrow neck and medium-sized chest. Make the stomach end in a point and add a belly button.

STEP 3 Add dark eyelashes and eyebrows above each eye. Now sketch a long mermaid tail that curves up and to the right.

STEP 4 Give Marina big, flowing hair that twists down the right side. Add a cute little sea star to hold the twists in place at the end. Then draw a tiny nose and curved mouth along the vertical guideline.

STEP 5 Erase the facial guidelines carefully. Then erase the line of the head that is covered by hair.

STEP 6 Add two fins to the end of the tail. Now give your mermaid two arms. Make the left arm bend upward and the right arm pointing to the side.

STEP 7 Erase the line of the tail that the fingers cover. Draw a scalloped seashell top on the chest. Add a few accessories like bracelets and a seashell necklace.

STEP 8 Cover your mermaid's tail with scales. Then shade in the tail fins, the top edge of the tail and the seashell top. Add more detail to the eyes. Finally, lightly shade Marina's hair. Draw a few more stars in her hair.

Practice Your Marina Skills!

Continue drawing Marina until she's as sleek as the water she glides through. Then she'll be ready to sing her siren's song!

Keep going from Step 1.

Try a few from scratch.

 LILITH (THE DEVIL)

Maybe you thought the devil was a big, ugly creature with a spiked tail and sharp teeth. But don't let Lilith's small stature and teasing grin fool you. With her trusty pitchfork and mischievous attitude, you'll see just how devious Lilith can be!

STEP 1
Draw a round head with a shallow indent along the left side. Sketch horizontal and vertical facial guidelines that are slightly curved and meet in the lower middle of the head.

STEP 2
Sketch two large eyes that rest on the horizontal guideline. Follow the horizontal guideline to the right edge of the head and draw a long, skinny ear. Then add a small body that ends in a point.

STEP 3
Draw a heart-shaped neckline on the body and add a skirt that ends in a few points. Then draw some dark eyelashes and eyebrows above the eyes.

STEP 4
Sketch long locks of hair atop the head and flowing down the sides. Make sure to add some bangs. Then draw a small, open mouth.

STEP 5
Erase the facial guidelines and the line of the head that is now covered by hair. Then add a tiny nose, two arms held up and to the sides, and two booted legs. Add long, sweeping sleeves to each arm.

STEP 6

Carefully erase some lines so that the hair overlaps the right sleeve and the right sleeve slightly overlaps the skirt. Then add a sharp pitchfork to the left hand.

STEP 7

Draw two devil horns on the top of the head. Then add a necklace and the edge of a wing peeking out of the hair on Lilith's right side.

STEP 8

Add dark shading to the horns, pitchfork, dress, necklace, wing, and boots. Give the eyes some definition by coloring in pupils and lightly shaded irises.

Sketch a Few More Liliths!

Practice your Lilith drawing skills until you master the basics. Then Lilith will be ready to fly off this page and rule the world of evil!

Keep going from Step 1.

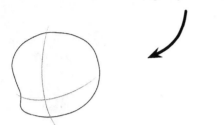

Try a few from scratch.

SANDY (THE SCHOOLGIRL)

Sandy enjoys school as much as the next kid, but she's always ready for some fun to give her a break from studying. With adventurous spirit and brainpower, Sandy is ready to ace her way across this page!

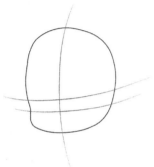

STEP 1
Draw a round, slightly lumpy head. Give the left side a small indent near the bottom of the face. Draw horizontal and vertical guidelines that meet in the middle of the head. Add a second horizontal line underneath the first.

STEP 2
Draw large eyes centered on the first horizontal guideline and resting on the second horizontal guideline. Then draw a narrow neck that flows into a short-sleeved shirt.

STEP 3
Add some dark eyelashes and eyebrows above the eyes. Then draw a short, flowing skirt.

STEP 4
Sketch two arms coming out of the sleeves. Then draw two legs that come together in a point. Add a tiny nose and a small, open mouth below the eyes and to the right of the vertical guideline.

STEP 5
Erase the facial guidelines and add wavy locks of hair that come down to the shoulders. Sketch some hair on the forehead and framing the sides of the face. Now add a small curl to the very top of the head.

STEP 6

Give the shirt some detail by adding a pocket, tie, collar, and an edge to the sleeves. Draw a belt around the skirt and add some socks and shoes. Then sketch a large bow on the right side of the head and the edge of another bow just peeking out on the left side.

STEP 7

Erase the lines of hair the big bow is covering up.

STEP 8

Finish Sandy by adding all the fun details! Apply some shading to her hair, tie, skirt, socks, and shoes. Give her eyes dark pupils and lightly shaded irises. Then complete Sandy's look by adding some polka dots to her bows!

Make Sandy Flawless!

Create some more Sandys below until you're sure you could get an A+ in drawing Sandy the Schoolgirl!

Keep going from Step 1.

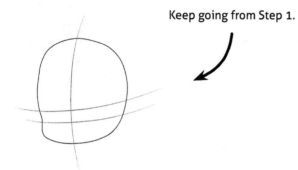

Try a few from scratch.

NYMPHADORA (THE NYMPH)

Nymphadora is part of an enchanted forest that lures people and animals in with its beauty and magic. This nymph spends her days flitting through the trees and singing to nature. Now she's ready to flutter her way across this page!

STEP 1
Draw a rounded head that has an indent along the left side of the head. Make the chin come to a slight point. Sketch horizontal and vertical facial guidelines that are slightly curved and meet in the center of the lower face.

STEP 2
Draw a long, pointed elf ear that sticks straight out of the right side of the head. Then add two large, round eyes that rest on the horizontal guideline.

STEP 3

Sketch a body that starts with a narrow neck, widens into shoulders and a small chest, indents slightly at the waist, and then flares wide into a flowing, ruffled skirt. Add dark eyelashes and eyebrows above each eye.

STEP 4

Draw hair around the top of the head that falls into wavy strands to the top of the skirt. Add some bangs around the face and a small curl atop the head. Now draw two tiny points along the vertical guideline for a nose and mouth.

STEP 5

Carefully erase the facial guidelines and the top line of the head. Then draw large ruffled sleeves coming out of the shoulders.

STEP 6

Erase the lines of hair and skirt that the new sleeves are now covering up. Add two legs and feet below the skirt.

STEP 7

Draw an adorable flower crown around your nymph's head. Then draw two long, narrow wings. Add a small necklace and anklet for some more cute details.

STEP 8

Erase the lines of hair covered by the right wing. Then bring Nymphadora to life by giving her some color. Lightly shade her dress and hair. Color in dark pupils and irises, and then add some more details to the flowers around her head.

Create the Perfect Nymphadora!

Drawing Nymphadora again and again will only make her more beautiful. Use the space below to practice until she's ready to fly off this page!

Keep going from Step 1.

Try a few from scratch.

ELFINA (THE FAIRY)

Elfina is perfectly cute and happy on most days. She loves to fly around and grant people's wishes if they've been good. But if she comes across someone being bad, you'll see how quickly Elfina will turn from a sweet fairy into a wicked pixie!

STEP 1 Begin by sketching a round head that indents slightly on the left side. Add some horizontal and vertical facial guidelines that meet in the lower center of the head.

STEP 2 Add two large eyes that rest on the horizontal guideline. Then give Elfina some blunt bangs across the forehead. Add more hair surrounding the top of the head and flowing down into curls. Now sketch a small body with a narrow neck, small shoulders, and a rounded chest.

STEP 3 Erase the line separating the bangs from the rest of the hair. Draw a long, pointed ear emerging from the hair on the right side of the face. Add eyelashes and eyebrows to each eye before moving down and sketching a wide, short skirt with a jagged edge.

STEP 4 Draw a tiny nose and small smile. Then give your fairy two arms, with the left bent up toward the shoulder. Add two legs underneath the skirt. Make the left leg cross under the right leg.

STEP 5 Erase the lines that the right and left arms are now covering up. Now carefully erase the facial guidelines.

STEP 6 Draw two angelic wings coming out from the shoulders. Add a thin ribbon that curls behind the waist and flows out to the sides of the body.

STEP 7 Sketch a beaded halo above Elfina's head and add a flower to her hair. Next, erase the lines of the wings that overlap the hair so the hair appears on top. Add a neckline to the chest and draw a necklace above. Then draw some vertical lines on the skirt to make it more ruffled, and add two small slippers to her feet.

STEP 8 Give some shading to Elfina's clothes, shoes, and hair. Make the ribbon around her darker. Finally, finish your fairy by filling out the eyes with dark pupils and lightly shaded irises.

Keep Drawing Elfina!

Draw Elfina until she's the best she can be. You can even try making her into that wicked pixie she turns into when she gets upset!

Keep going from Step 1.

Try a few from scratch.

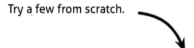

PRACTICE PAGE

DRAWING CHIBI

PRACTICE PAGE

Discover More Great How-to-Draw Books from Ulysses Press

Learn more at www.ulyssespress.com

Printed in the USA
CPSIA information can be obtained
at www.ICGtesting.com
LVHW081731241123
764291LV00006B/26

9 781646 040933